AF394079

FRANCISCO GOYA

A true artistic visionary

With Marie-Julie Malache
In collaboration with Elisabeth Bruyns
Translated by Soline de Dorlodot

Art & Literature 50MINUTES.com

FRANCISCO GOYA

- **Name:** Francisco de Goya y Lucientes.
- **Born:** 30 March 1746 in Fuendetodos (Spain).
- **Died:** 16 April 1828 in Bordeaux (France).
- **Context:** the spread of the ideas of the Enlightenment, the beginnings of Romanticism and the Napoleonic Wars in Spain.
- **Notable works:**
  - *The Adoration of the Name of God* (1772), fresco
  - *The Sleep of Reason Produces Monsters*, etching belonging to the *Los Caprichos* series (c. 1797)
  - *Witches' Sabbath* (1797-1798), painting
  - *The Nude Maja* (1795-1800), painting
  - *Charles IV of Spain and His Family* (1800-1801), painting
  - *The Clothed Maja* (1800-1807), painting
  - *The Third of May 1808* (1814), painting
  - *Saturn Devouring His Son* (1821), painting

Francisco Goya is one of Spain's most important artists, along with illustrious figures such as

Diego Velásquez (1599-1660) and Pablo Picasso (1881-1973). He lived through a period of major social and political upheaval, and this challenge to traditional values is expressed in his art. His extensive body of work, featuring oil paintings, murals, etchings, lithographs and drawings, reveals a daring style, an innovate approach to art and a fascinating creative force.

Goya's life and work were both full of contradictions. As the highest-ranking painter at the Spanish court, he faithfully depicted the ostentatious riches of the Spanish aristocracy. Indeed, his talents as a portraitist were recognised from the beginning of his career, and this royal patronage allowed him to secure commissions from the highest levels of the Spanish nobility later on. However, at the same time he used his personal works (mainly etchings) to denounce social injustice and human weakness. He was influenced in this by the Enlightenment ideals which had reached Spain and were inspiring writers, historians and politicians who wanted to modernise Spanish society. As such, in one of the less enlightened countries of Europe, Goya became a liberal thinker as well as a critical painter.

His work, which aims to provide a detailed analysis of human nature, expresses the universality of suffering.

Nowadays, art historians often struggle to classify Goya's work, as these two sides – court painter and critical witness – resulted in groundbreaking original compositions. The considerable variety of his style also makes attempts at classification difficult.

CONTEXT

DARK YEARS IN SPAIN

Goya's works are fiery and violent, and at times tormented, in terms of both theme and style. This can be explained by the political, ideological, social and economic context that the artist lived through, as this was a very difficult period for Spain.

In the early 19th century, the deeply conservative nation entered a phase of political and social decline, and its people became increasingly poor. On 21 October 1805, the British destroyed the combined Spanish and French fleet at the Battle of Trafalgar. Following this disastrous defeat, Spain lost its status as a maritime superpower, and was also cut off from its American colonies, depriving the country of important markets. In 1806, the Spanish Crown agreed to support Napoleon I (1769-1821) in his invasion of Portugal: French troops were allowed to march through Spain, which was consequently overrun by thousands of soldiers. Two years later, King Charles IV (1748-

1819) abdicated in favour of his son Ferdinand VII (1784-1833) and fled to Bayonne in the south of France. Napoleon I then invited Ferdinand VII to Bayonne and persuaded him to give the crown back to his father. After he agreed, the young king was imprisoned. Charles IV then abdicated in favour of Napoleon I, who gave the Spanish throne to his brother Joseph Bonaparte (1768-1844) in June 1808. However, many Spaniards refused to accept their new leader and decided to resist: an insurrection then broke out and spread across most of the country. During the six years that followed, violent conflicts erupted between the supporters of the Spanish monarchy and the *afrancesados*, who supported the French in the hope that they would bring a more enlightened regime. Spain became a battlefield dominated by violence and fear. Goya bore witness to the atrocities of the conflict in a series of etchings called *The Disasters of War*, in which he illustrated the cruelty of the human race.

In 1812, British forces invaded Spain and drove out Joseph Bonaparte and the French army. The Spanish parliament then tried to establish a constitutional monarchy. However, Ferdinand VII returned to power, enthusiastically supported by the population, and set up an autocratic regime. He restored the Inquisition, dissolved the parliament and had everybody who had supported the French government imprisoned.

THE IDEALS OF THE ENLIGHTENMENT

The Age of Enlightenment in the 18th century was characterised by significant ideological, political, scientific, economic and social progress, which paved the way for the French Revolution in 1789. The ideas of this movement were transmitted by philosophers, scientists, writers and artists, and soon spread across Europe (with the exception of Spain). The movement's proponents advocated the use of reason to access knowledge and, through knowledge, happiness. They believed in the value of critical thinking and distanced themselves from traditions and the political and religious authorities of the time. They denounced absolute monarchy and the excesses of the ecclesiastic institutions, and advocated the separation of Church and State. A form of committed literature emerged, with writers such as Montesquieu (1684-1755), Voltaire (1694-1778) and Denis Diderot (1713-1784) in France. Meanwhile, artists looked back to Antiquity as a model of objectivity and simplicity in terms of both subject and style, giving rise to Neoclassicism.

BETWEEN NEOCLASSICISM AND ROMANTICISM

Goya was at the crossroads of several artistic movements. Although Baroque tendencies were still present at the beginning of the 18th century – Goya's early murals were largely inspired by this aesthetic – from the second half of the century onwards, under the influence of Enlightenment philosophy, Neoclassicism spread widely through academic teaching, advocating a refined and controlled kind of art. However, at the end of the 18th century, in reaction to the rationalism of the Enlightenment, some artists decided to give free rein to their creativity, and used their work to demonstrate their subjectivity, imagination and feelings. This movement, which flourished in Germany with painters such as Caspar David

Friedrich (1774-1840), was given the name Romanticism and influenced all forms of art. The favourite themes of the German Romantics were melancholy, loneliness, the almighty nature and nostalgia for the past, in particular for an imaginary and idealised Middle Ages.

At the beginning of the 19th century, Romanticism spread to the rest of Europe. In France, the main representatives of this movement were Théodore Géricault (1791-1824) and Eugène Delacroix (1798-1863). Their works provoked a scandal at the Salon (the official exhibition) because of the use of colour and movement in their compositions, which were wholly at odds with Neoclassicism. Indeed, while Neoclassical works typically featured precisely delineated drawings, Romantic paintings were dominated by vibrant splashes of colour.

In the United Kingdom, the main representatives of Romanticism were William Turner (1775-1851) and John Constable (1776-1837), who painted mainly landscapes. On the whole, the Romantic artists had a considerable influence on modern painting with their bleak, tormented compositions.

ENGRAVING AND LITHOGRAPHY

Goya was one of the pioneers of lithography, a new printing technique developed between 1796 and 1799 by the Austrian inventor Aloys Senefelder (1771-1834). This process of serial reproduction is based on the principle of that oil and water do not mix. Originally, this invention interested mainly printers of music scores and maps. As can be deduced from its name, a stone (*litho*) is used, on which a drawing (*graph*) is made using a greasy substance. Unlike engraving on brass plates, lithography does not require any training: the practitioner must simply master the principle of "mirror" drawing (the printing is carried out by turning the stone on the paper). Moreover, lithography allows many copies of the same drawing to be printed, which explains the technique's incredible success.

PRINTING

Printing is a technique which has been used throughout the entire history of art, from the application of hands covered in pigments to the walls of prehistoric caves to the screenprints produced by Andy Warhol (1928-1987). This technique requires two surfaces – one bearing the image, one on which the image will be printed. Two different forms of printing can be distinguished: relief printing and intaglio printmaking. With relief printing (on clay, wood, linoleum), the printing surface is in relief, while the rest of the support, hollowed out with the help of a chisel or gouge (a kind of curved chisel) will not appear on the print. Relief printing was progressively replaced by intaglio engraving, in which incisions are made on a metal plaque (brass, zinc, or steel) with the help of a dry point or chisel. The entire plaque is covered in ink, then wiped so that ink remains only in the engraved incisions. The printing is completed with strong pressure, so that the paper comes into contact with the inked lines. Later, artists experimented with chemical techniques, using acid to draw on the metal plaque. In the case of etching, for example, the metal plaque is first covered with a varnish which resists the acid. The drawing is then done with a point which takes the varnish away without scratching the plaque. The plaque is subsequently immersed into an acid bath which attacks the exposed metal. This technique is often combined with that of aquatint, which allows semi-tints to be obtained. This is done by projecting resin onto the plaque and using heat to set it. When the plaque is immersed in the acid, only the zones of bare metal around each resinous particle are attacked.

BIOGRAPHY

FOLLOWING IN THE FOOTSTEPS OF THE ITALIAN MASTERS

Francisco Goya, the son of José Goya and Gracia Lucientes, was born in 1746 in Fuendetodos (Zaragoza) to a modest family. As a teenager, he tried his hand at painting in the workshop of José Luzán Martinez (1710-1785). This local religious painter mainly had him copy engravings of the great masters. He followed his lessons with three talented brothers: Francisco (1734-1795), Manuel (1740-1809) and Ramón Bayeu (1746-1793).

At the time, on a cultural level, Zaragoza and the region of Aragón were dependent on Madrid, where the Academy of Fine Arts, created in 1752, set the rules of artistic creation and defined good taste. In 1763 and 1766, Goya signed up for the competition to enter the Academy, but was unsuccessful: his fieriness repulsed the jury, which preferred more sober and quiet compositions.

At the age of 20, like the other young artists of

his time, he travelled to Italy to get inspiration from the great masters. For five years, he lived in Naples, Rome and Palermo, where he discovered Roman Neoclassicism. In the spring of 1771, he signed up for the competition run by the Academy of Palermo and obtained six votes, but no award. Goya then headed for Zaragoza, where he received his first major commissions. From 1772 to 1774, in the Basilica of Our Lady of the Pillar (Zaragoza) and then in the Carthusian monastery of Aula Dei (a few miles from the city), he created his first masterpieces, murals with religious themes, the styles of which were clearly inspired by his Italian training.

PAINTING FOR THE NOBILITY

In 1773, Goya, aged 27, married Josefa Bayeu, the sister of his painter friends. This marriage may be seen as a form of recognition of his talents as a painter: as both of Josefa's parents were dead, it was her eldest brother, Francisco Bayeu, who granted Goya her hand in marriage. She bore Goya several children, most of whom died at an early age. His son Francisco Javier, born in 1784, was the only one to survive.

His marriage to Josefa gave his career a boost, as his brothers-in-law obtained commissions for him from the Royal Tapestry Factory of Santa Barbara, which ensured him stable work. He produced tapestries in which he represented the parties and entertainments of the young people of Madrid, depicting their contagious love for life and carefree happiness. In his many works, including *La Gallina Ciega* ("Blind Man's Bluff", 1791), he portrayed people with very lively expressions and used bright colours. Before long, the success of Goya's tapestries propelled Goya into the world of the Spanish nobility.

TAPESTRY

A tapestry is a large, flat piece of fabric made to be hung inside or outside. It usually represents past or current events (which may be religious, political or historical), but can also bear purely decorative motifs. It is hung on a wall and provides both heat and noise insulation. Tapestries are usually produced as a series: each of them then represents an episode of the story told by the whole series. From the Middle Ages, the technique has consisted of three stages:

the artist draws a small-scale preparatory drawing, then the model is made in the size of the final tapestry and, finally, a weaver weaves the tapestry on a loom. Tapestries were usually meant for wealthier citizens, meaning nobles and clergymen, as well as the better-off member of the bourgeoisie on occasion.

To complete his training, Goya began to engrave the paintings of Velásquez towards the end of the 1770s. He therefore played a part in the diffusion of the works of this great Spanish painter, whilst learning how to create the magical atmosphere that characterised his work. He discovered how to suggest a face, a shimmering fabric or a jewel with a spot and a few impastos. Goya's prints were published in a Madrid newspaper in July and December 1778.

Two years later, in 1780, the artist made another attempt at the entry competition to the Academy of San Fernando, with a work on an uncontroversial subject: *Christ on the Cross*. For its style, he chose the chiaroscuro popularised by Caravaggio (c. 1571-1610). Although this work was traditional and lacked originality, it secured his entry to the Academy by unanimous vote. He quickly rose through the ranks and was appointed sub-director of the painting department in 1785.

His fame as a portraitist of the nobility also grew quickly. The following year, he was promoted to court painter. In this position, he painted his *Portrait of Charles III in Hunting Costume*. This king was renowned for his ugliness, and Goya did not try to idealise his traits in the least. Moreover, wanting to match his name to his new function, Goya added the nobiliary particle 'de' to it. In 1788, he became Charles IV's chamber painter and, in 1799, became his first painter. This period of his life was mainly defined by his court portraits, but also by several portraits of his friends in high society.

EXPLORING THE DARK SIDE OF HUMANITY

However, in the early 1790s Goya lost his hearing following a serious illness. As a consequence, the way he perceived his environment changed and he started looking more critically at the world. He then developed an interest in the dark side of human nature and explored the supernatural world, haunted by fantastical characters and frightening creatures. Moreover, he spent time with thinkers inspired by the Enlightenment, who influenced him and sharpened his critical point of view. He then made a series of 80 aquatinted etchings under the title *Los Caprichos*. Published in 1799, these etchings illustrated moral tragedies, ignorance and foolish, and also featured subtle political allusions. This series marked a new turning point in Goya's career.

The Peninsular War (1808-1814) further fuelled his reflections on humanity. Horrified by the behaviour of the warring parties, he drew sketches based on his observations, which he later developed into a series of etchings entitled *The Disasters of War*. At the same time, he also continued his work of social criticism, in particular with *Yard with Lunatics* (1808-1812), a painting in which he denounced the living conditions of those suffering from mental illness.

However, Goya generally stayed away from politics; he was more preoccupied with his career. This was why he accepted a position as official painter to the French king. He then made paintings of French officers such as the general Nicolas Guye (1773-1845), Commander of the Royal Order of the Two Sicilies and of the Royal Order of Spain. This work would cost Goya dearly, as at the end of the war he was accused of collaboration by the court of the Inquisition. Stating that he had painted Joseph Bonaparte on the basis of engravings and not from life, he was quickly acquitted. He even returned to his position at Ferdinand VII's side, as the king was happy to keep such a well-known artist in his employment.

However, Goya progressively distanced himself from the court. He became increasingly withdrawn, and developed an interest in madness and superstitions. In his house, known as the *Quinta del Sordo* ("House of the Deaf Man"), he painted powerful and dark images, inhabited by sinister characters. He painted directly on the plaster of the walls with oil paint. In 1837, these works were transferred onto canvases; they are now on display at the Prado Museum in Madrid. Moreover, the political instability in Spain disappointed Goya and prompted him to leave for Paris, on the pretext of his health. He settled in Bordeaux in 1824, where he met with other Spanish intellectuals in exile. The publication of the *La Tauromaquia* series of lithographs in 1825 attests to his fondness for bullfighting, despite his advanced age. He died in 1828, at the age of 82, leaving behind roughly 1000 oil paintings and murals, nearly 300 etchings and lithographs, and thousands of drawings.

CHARACTERISTICS OF GOYA'S WORK

BETWEEN TRADITION AND MODERNITY

"I had three teachers: Velásquez, Rembrandt, and nature." This quotation, attributed to Goya, perfectly summarises the fusion of traditional influences and original artistic inventions in his work.

While studying the works of Velásquez, he learned how to imitate the variations of colours in lights in order to obtain a clear relief without resorting to violent contrasts between lights and shadow. Like him, Goya played with the transparency of colours and a sober colour range (ochres, white, black, very little red and blue, in judicious touches). His perception of light was also influenced by Rembrandt (1606-1669). Following the example of this northern master, he used traditional painting techniques: he prepared his canvas carefully, chose and mixed his colours, applied impastos and glazes (very fluid, translucent liquids, which are applied in a very thin and uniform layer in order to modify the background against which they are applied). This means that his paintings are very well-preserved and their colours have not altered much with time.

However, aside from these sources of inspiration, Goya brought an innovative touch to his works. Although he received formal artistic training, he distanced himself from classical art by introducing spontaneity into his creations. Thanks to a fiery pictorial style (as opposed to the sobriety promoted by academic painting), he managed to raise daily life to the same level as historical topics, whilst retaining its naturalness and gaiety. His characters, far from looking frozen, feel as if they are real flesh-and-blood people. In 1792, Goya affirmed this search for originality, stating that "there are no rules in painting". By this, he meant that students had to choose their sources of inspiration themselves and develop their artistic technique freely.

AN UNPARALLELED PORTRAITIST

Although Goya's work deals with numerous topics (religious art, war scenes, illustration of the barbarism of war, fantastical imagination), it was mainly thanks to his portraits that he established his reputation. Gifted with the ability to capture the personality of his models rather than just copying their physical features, he was interested in the psychology of his models and tried to show the truth behind the faces he painted on canvas.

The balance in his portraits and self-portraits reveals the thoughtfulness of his compositions and his impressive knowledge of anatomy. Moreover, his keen sense of observation allowed him to depict the intricacies of embroideries and lace with precision and finesse. He also tried to represent the different social types with realism and authenticity, as much in their attitudes as in their clothing. Despite his official commissions and the need to conform to the wishes of his patrons, Goya was confident enough to interpret his subjects in a daring and inventive way.

THE ROLE OF THE FANTASTIC

In his personal works, Goya produced engravings haunted by creatures straight out of his imagination: bats, owls and cats stand side by side with elves, demons, ghosts, goats and witches. The black and white of the prints create strong contrasts which strengthen the dramatic tension of the scenes depicted. These usually take the form of a satire or a caricature in which exaggerated emotions, such as fear or repulsion, take centre stage.

However, Goya's frightening creatures must above all be considered as allegories of human behaviour, with the aim of formulating a critique or making an ideological allusion. The artist chose this method to criticise, among other things, the oppression of poor workers by the idle and unproductive aristocrats. In terms of the tone of these works, he managed to preserve a delicate balance between moralising and a comedy of manners.

Nevertheless, it is hard to interpret Goya's engravings in more detail as he used proverbs, rhetorical figures and sayings. This is why the meaning of some of his prints still eludes us, enhancing the mystery of these dark works.

NOTABLE WORKS

THE ADORATION OF THE NAME OF GOD

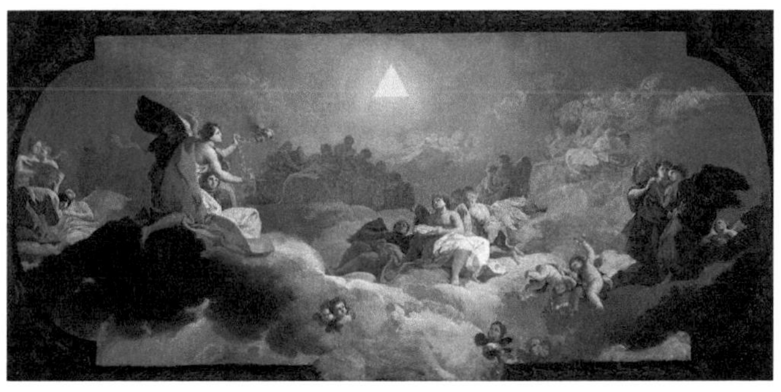

| *The Adoration of the Name of God*, 1772, fresco, 700 x 1500 cm, Zaragoza, Basilica of Our Lady of the Pillar.

Shortly after his return from Italy, Goya received a prestigious commission from the Basilica of Our Lady of the Pillar in Zaragoza. The building was being remodelled in a Neoclassical style, and he was tasked with decorating the vault over the small choir of the Virgin Chapel. To prove his technical mastery, Goya presented a sketch and a draft of an oil painting. These were immediately accepted and the artist was granted permission begin working. This work laid the foundations for his later career.

This fresco glorifies the triumphant Church. At its centre, the name of God is written in Hebrew in a triangle representing the Trinity. A bright golden colour emerges from the background to bathe the scene in light. This creates shadows on the clouds from the viewer's perspective and is reflected in the silk clothing. The fresco's composition is extremely rigorous: the crowd of angels floating on the clouds follows the lines of concentric semi-circles. The perspective echoes this composition by drawing the spectator's eye towards the triangle with the name of God. Each detail strengthens this impression, such as the movement of the angels on the right of the fresco as they swing a censer. In addition, the lightness and innocence of the *putti* in the foreground give spectators the feeling that they are penetrating into the space of the work.

In this early work, Goya's style is close to that of the late Baroque era due to its diaphanous colour and use of reflection. That said, in spite of the rapid brushstrokes, the piece as a whole is fairly static, unlike Baroque compositions. However, it is worth mentioning that the fresco currently displayed in the Basilica of Our Lady of the Pillar has undergone four restorations. Compared to the artist's earlier drawings and sketches, the final project appears less daring and dynamic than the original.

CHARLES IV OF SPAIN AND HIS FAMILY

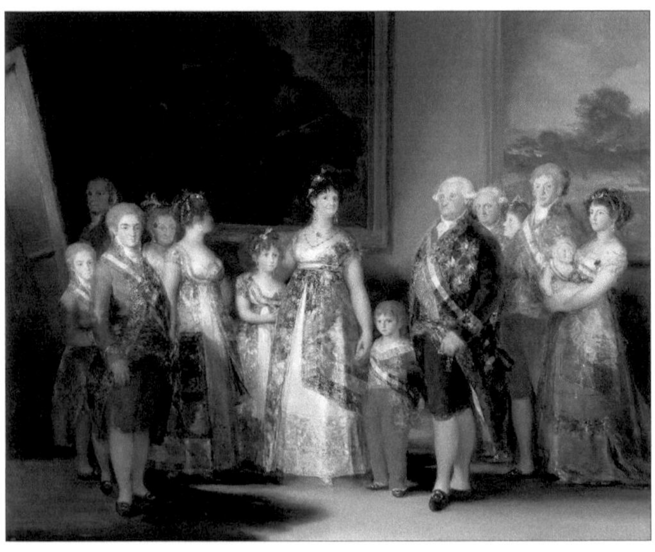

| *Charles IV and His Family*, 1800-1801, oil painting on canvas, 280 x 336 cm, Madrid, Prado Museum.

As the court painter, Goya was asked to depict the members of the royal family in a monumental life-size group portrait. The composition is traditional and well thought out, with the characters placed hierarchically. At the centre are the King Charles IV and Queen Maria Luisa (1751-1819) with their two youngest children. The queen's arms are bare, as are those of the other ladies in the painting. Indeed, the queen was known for having forbidden the wearing of gloves at court, because she liked her arms so much that she did want to hide them. On the left of the portrait, in blue, the heir to the throne, Ferdinand VII, mirrors his father's pose. His other brother, the Infante Carlos (1788-1855), is beside him. On his other side is Ferdinand VII's future wife, depicted with her face hidden because at the time of the portrait the engagement was not yet official. Between the young couple, Doña Maria Josefa (1744-1801), the king's sister, can be seen. On the right-hand side of the painting, close relatives are represented: the king's brother, the Infante Antonio Pascual (1755-1817); his eldest daughter, the Infanta Doña Carlota Joaquina (1775-1830); and, with a child in her arms, another daughter, the Infanta Maria Luisa (1782-1824), close to her husband, Louis I of Etruria (1773-1803). In the background on the left, the artist has depicted himself, painting on a canvas – a *mise en abyme* borrowed from Velásquez, who had done the same in the painting *Las Meninas* (1656). The painter is focused and has his gaze directed at the viewer, as if he were observing the group in a mirror.

The scene is lit by an artificial light originating from outside of the painting, on the left. It creates contrasts between the parts in the light and the parts in the shadows. The golds and blacks of the colour palette echo this contrast.

Although Goya follows the traditional rules of composition and lighting in this painting, his style and the way he depicts the faces are surprising: although the jewels and clothes are luxurious, the faces are dull, pretentious and even arrogant. In the 19th century, Théophile Gautier (1811-1872) compared the characters in the painting to "the corner baker and his wife after they won the lottery". The realism of this painting is all the more surprising when we find out that the royal family did not object to it.

THE NUDE MAJA

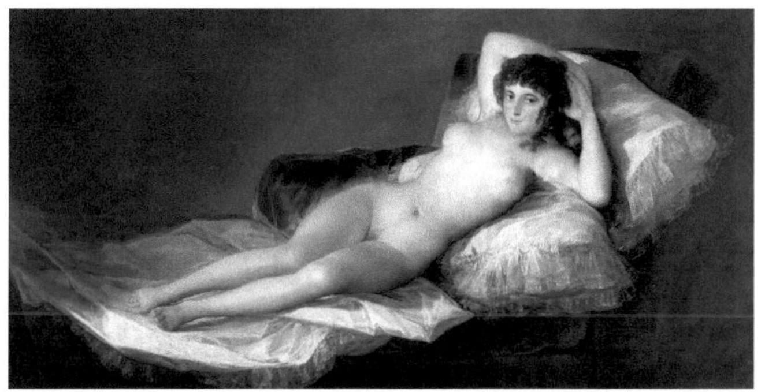

| *The Nude Maja*, 1795-1800, oil painting on canvas, 98 x 191 cm. Madrid, Prado Museum

The painting depicts a young Spanish woman lying on a bed covered in silk pillows, entirely naked and with her arms and elbows lifted to the same height as her face. She gazes seductively at the spectator, inviting them to contemplate the voluptuous form of her body. This was more than enough for *The Nude Maja* to trigger a scandal and for the Inquisition to accuse this painting and its artist of obscenity and immorality. It was primarily due to the disapproval of the Church that nudity seldom appeared in Spanish art. To circumvent this interdiction, Spanish painters usually depicted mythological scenes featuring naked goddesses, but in Goya's work, the young woman is not a divine figure: she is a *maja* (a young woman of modest condition) who exists in real life.

This painting was commissioned by the "Prince of Peace", Manuel Godoy y Álvarez de Faria (1767-1852), a protégé of the queen Maria Luisa. Historians offer two hypotheses as to the identity of the model: she could be the Duchess of Alba, with whom Goya was on fairly intimate terms, but the most widely accepted theory is that the young *maja* is Godoy's mistress, the actress Pepita Tudó. Originally, the painting was exhibited in Godoy's paintings cabinet, next to its companion piece, *The Clothed Maja* (1800-18007). Nobody knows which painting was made first. However, the identical pose and décor are proof that they are linked. Moreover, the clothed young lady is just as provocative as the naked one, from the curves which can be seen under her clothes to the sensuality of her pose. It can even be supposed that *The Clothed Maja* was exhibited superimposed on *The Nude Maja* and that a mechanism would slide down the upper portrait to reveal the naked portrait, as this type of recreational entertainment was highly fashionable in the painting cabinets of the time.

The Nude Maja has been stored in the Prado Museum since 1910. Before that, it was exhibited along with other daring nudes at the Academy of San Fernando. In 1930, it caused a new scandal, when postage stamps featuring the image were issued.

THE SLEEP OF REASON PRODUCES MONSTERS

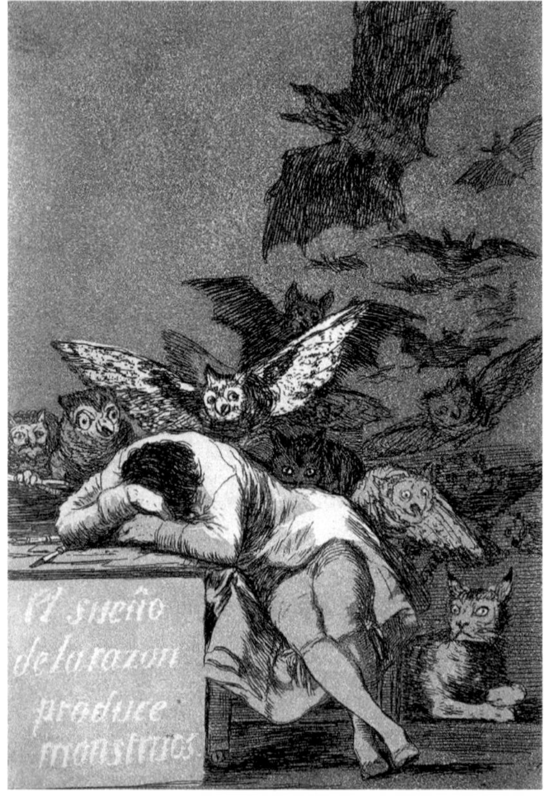

| *The Sleep of Reason Produces Monsters*, etching belonging to the *Los Caprichos* series, c. 1797, 21.6 x 15.2 cm, private collection.

At the end of the 18th century, Goya gave free rein to his taste for the fantastic in a collection of drawings entitled *Dreams*. Later, he perfected and engraved them, turning them into a series of 80 etchings called *Los Caprichos* and offering them for sale in February 1799. *The Sleep of Reason Produces Monsters* appears in the middle of the series, after satirical images of society and as an introduction to the theme of witchcraft.

The etching depicts an artist who has fallen asleep on a table covered with paper and pencils, allowing his subconscious to take over. Around this character Goya shows the nightmare which is playing in his mind: creatures come out of the shadows and circle him while a lynx observes what is happening. At the centre, a black cat stares with large, hostile eyes. The use of etching is effective, because the black and white create sharp contrasts which emphasise the dark atmosphere of the scene.

The drawing can be interpreted in two different ways: on the one hand, the artist may simply have wanted to express the strength of the imagination when it is not held back by reason; on the other hand, the nightmare suggests that the character is despairing and unable to continue his work. The location of this etching in the series seems to corroborate this second theory: unable to find truth through reason, the artist is drawn to the fantastic and the surreal as a form of escape.

THE THIRD OF MAY 1808

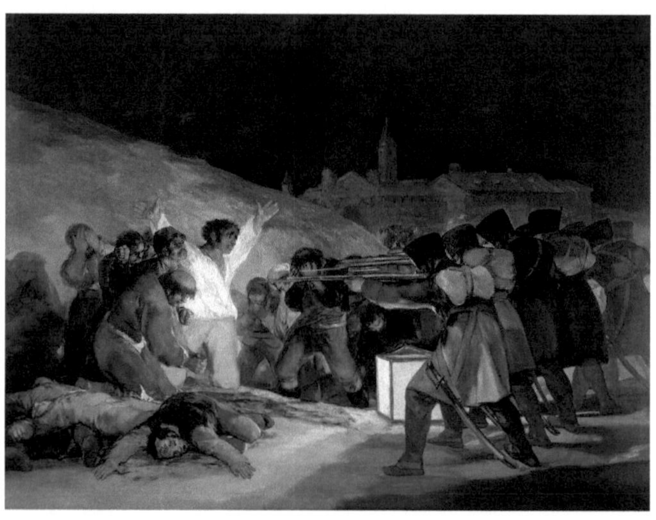

| *The Third of May 1808*, 1814, oil painting on canvas, 268 x 347 cm, Madrid, Prado museum.

This famous work by Goya illustrates a dark episode in Spanish history. On 3 May 1808, on the hill of the Príncipe Pío, the French army executed Spanish patriots in retaliation for their uprising against the occupation the previous day. Some 40 men and women were executed. This painting was very influential in the 19th century because it respects the norms of traditional painting while depicting a novel subject. Goya portrays the tension and fear in the moments immediately prior to the execution of an ordinary man.

In a nocturnal atmosphere, the central character immediately draws our attention: wearing a white shirt, he opens the arms. His face and gestures suggest that he faces death with a mixture of courage and despair. The light coming from the lantern in front of the firing squad enhances the drama and tension of the scene. The heroism of this man is highlighted by his white clothing, which symbolises innocence, but also by the wound on his right hand, which recalls the Holy Wounds of Christ. The men surrounding him all react in their own way: a Franciscan priest bows his head, a man covers his eyes with his hands, another clenches his fists in a gesture of futile resistance. In the foreground of the painting, bullet-riddled corpses have fallen. The arms of the man covered in his own blood on the ground are an echo of those of the martyr standing behind him.

This scene represents just one moment, but what is to follow can already be guessed. When this group has fallen, it will be replaced by another one, which is already climbing the hill with heavy feet. Facing the victims, the soldiers are anonymous: they form a wall and their positions are identical. They are about to fire. Finally, despite the frozen aspect of the scene, the painting is noisy: the illusion of sound is strong, which adds to the overall tension.

GOYA'S LEGACY

Goya's talent was only truly appreciated after his death. When he died in 1828, the press did not even mention it. A quarter of a century elapsed before French painters gave him the outstanding place he now occupies in art history. With a style and subject choice that were both daring and full of contradictions, Goya came to be considered as one of the precursors of the pictorial avant-garde of the 19th and 20th centuries.

His influence can be clearly in the Romantic works by Eugène Delacroix. As a child, Delacroix discovered and appreciated the etchings of the Spanish artist. Moreover, the two artists had shared connections, as was highlighted by the 2014 exhibition *De Goya à Delacroix, les relations artistiques de la famille Guillemardet* ("From Goya to Delacroix. The artistic relationships of the Guillemardet family") at the Rolin Museum in Autun (Burgundy, France). Goya painted the portrait of the father, Ferdinand Guillemardet (1765-1809), who was the French ambassador in

Spain, whereas Delacroix produced a portrait of the son, Félix Guillemardet (1796-1842).

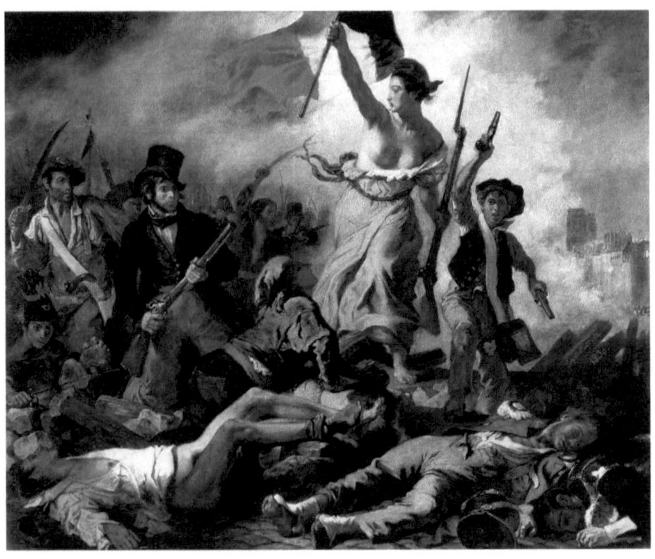

| Eugène Delacroix, *Liberty Leading the People*, 1830, oil painting on canvas, 260x325 cm, Paris, Louvre museum

Likewise, in Delacroix's *Liberty Leading the People* (1830), the celebration of the ordinary hero in a historical scene reminds us of the man in white shirt at the centre of *The Third of May 1808* by Goya. But beyond these thematic similarities, Delacroix mainly draws on Goya's dynamism and his fiery brushstrokes. However, the French painter goes even further by offering tormented compositions based on a violent use of colour.

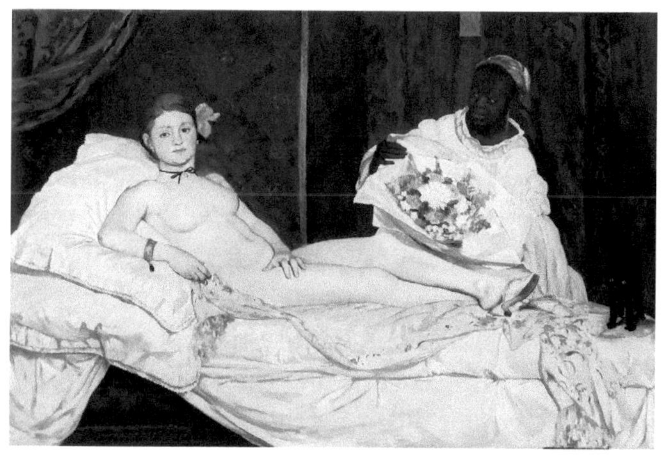

| Édouard Manet, *Olympia*, 1863, oil painting on canvas, 130.5 x 191 cm, Paris, Orsay Museum.

In the second half of the 19th century, Édouard Manet (1832-1883) caused a scandal with his painting *Olympia* (1863), which recalls *The Nude Maja* in terms of both form and iconography. Like the *maja*, the naked woman is lying on silk sheets and gazes provocatively at the spectator. However, Manet makes his model colder than Goya's: whereas the *maja* is a mistress, symbolising passionate love, Olympia is a prostitute. In this way, Manet's painting symbolises a corrupt form of love and contains an element of social criticism.

The other side of Goya's work, which was darker and more mysterious, has also influenced modern and contemporary artists. In 1857, in the French newspaper *Le Présent*, Charles Baudelaire (1821-1867) contributed to the Spanish painter's fame by underlining his taste for the fantastic and the horrifying. Impressed by his etchings in contrasting blacks and whites, the poet was also fascinated by witchcraft and the atmospheres of Sabbaths conjured up by the Spanish painters. The theme of the occult, which is omnipresent in modern painting, reached its peak in the 20th century in the works of the Surrealists. Following on from Goya, Salvador Dalí (1904-1989) depicted fantastic nightmares that could be both frightening and fascinating.

SUMMARY

- Francisco Goya, born in 1746, is a key figure in Spanish art history, alongside Velásquez and Picasso. His work is vast, on every level: he worked in multiple mediums (oil painting, frescoes, drawings, etchings, lithographs) and employed a wide range of subjects, themes and styles.
- As one of the main painters at the Spanish court, he received many official commissions, mainly portraits of the nobility. He had a gift for capturing the personality of the sitters, rather than just copying their physical features. His works are therefore defined by a great attention to reality.
- However, Goya was full of contradictions. In his personal works, he denounced human weakness and social injustice, turning himself into a witness of the political and ideological troubles of his time. His works then took the form of satires and caricatures populated by fantastic creatures which both fascinate and frighten.

- Nowadays, Goya is considered by art historians as a forerunner of the avant-garde movement of the 19th and 20th centuries. His influence on Eugène Delacroix and on modern painters such as Édouard Manet has been highlighted many times, while his taste for the fantastic is echoed in the paintings of the Surrealists.

FURTHER READING

BIBLIOGRAPHY

- Baticle, J. (1994) *Goya: Painter of Terror and Splendour*. London: Thames and Hudson.

- Charles, V. and Manca, J. (2008) Francisco de Goya. *1000 Paintings of Genius*. New York: Parkstone Press, pp. 272 and 522-523.

- (2004) *Francisco de Goya*. London: Sirocco.

- Hagen, R. and Hagen, M-R. (2016) *Goya*. Cologne: Taschen.

- Hofmann, W. (2014) *Goya. Du Ciel à l'Enfer en passant par le monde*. Paris: Hazan.

- Krausse, A-K. (2013) Le peintre de cour rebelle, Francisco de Goya. *Histoire de la peinture de la Renaissance à nos jours*. Paris: H. F. Ullmann.

- Marcheschi, J-P. (2012) *Goya. Voir l'obscur*. Paris: Art 3 Galerie.

- Restellini, M. (2013) *Goya et la modernité*. Paris: Pinacothèque.

- Todorov, T. (2011) *Goya à l'ombre des Lumières*. Paris: Flammarion.

ICONOGRAPHIC SOURCES

- *The Adoration of the Name of God*, 1772, fresco. Royalty-free reproduction picture.

- *Charles IV and His Family*, 1800-1801, oil painting on canvas. Royalty-free reproduction picture.

- *The Nude Maja*, 1795-1800, oil painting on canvas. Royalty-free reproduction picture.

- *The Sleep of Reason Produces Monsters*, etching belonging to the *Los Caprichos* series, c. 1797. Royalty-free reproduction picture.

- *The Third of May 1808*, 1814, oil painting on canvas. Royalty-free reproduction picture.

- *Liberty Leading the People*, 1830, oil painting on canvas. Royalty-free reproduction picture.

- *Olympia*, 1863, oil painting on canvas. Royalty-free reproduction picture.

Although the editor makes every effort to verify the accuracy of the information published, 50Minutes. com accepts no responsibility for the content of this book.

www.50minutes.com

Ebook EAN: 9782806272911

Paperback EAN: 9782808006552

Legal Deposit: D/2017/12603/886

Cover image: © *Sueño de San José* by Goya

Digital conception by Primento, the digital partner of publishers.